Alabama Bingo Book

COMPLETE BINGO GAME IN A BOOK

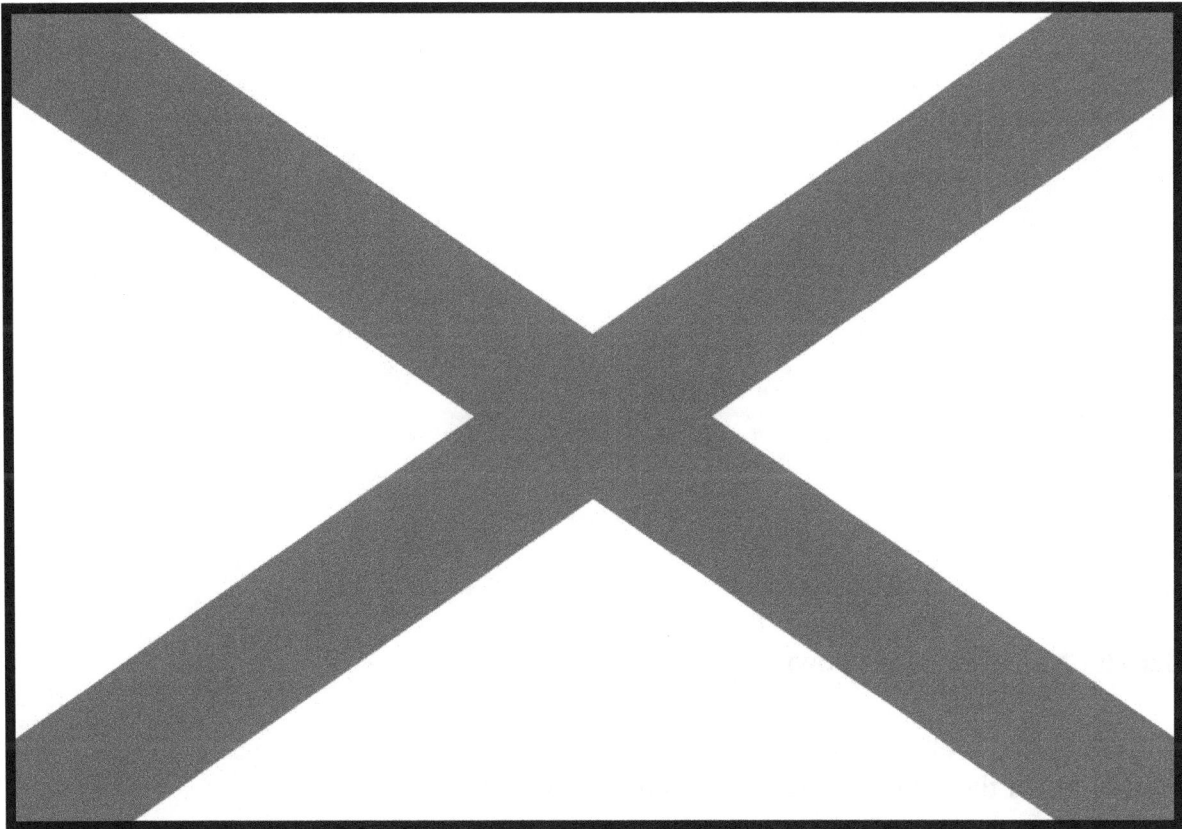

Written By Rebecca Stark
Educational Books 'n' Bingo

TITLE: Alabama Bingo
AUTHOR: Rebecca Stark

ISBN 978-0-87386-494-7

Educational Books 'n' Bingo

Printed in the U.S.A.

DIRECTIONS

1. **Either cut apart the book or make copies of ALL the sheets. You might want to make an extra copy of the clue sheets to use for introduction and review. Keep the sheets in an envelope for easy reuse.**

2. Cut apart the call sheets with terms and clues.

3. Pass out one bingo sheet per student. There are enough unique sheets for a class of 30.

4. Pass out the markers. You may cut apart the markers included in this book or use any other small items of your choice. Students can also mark the sheets themselves; recopy the sheets as needed for additional games.

5. Decide whether or not you will require the entire sheet to be filled. Requiring the entire sheet to be filled provides a better review. However, if you have a short time to fill, you may prefer to have them do the just the border or some other format. Tell the class before you begin what is required.

6. There are 50 terms. Read the list before you begin. If there are any terms that have not been covered in class, you may want to read to the students the term and clues before you begin.

7. There is a blank space in the middle of each sheet. You can instruct the students to use it as a free space or you can write in answers to cover terms not included. Of course, in this case you would create your own clues. (Templates provided.)

8. Shuffle the sheets and place them in a pile. Two or three clues are provided for each term. If you plan to play the game with the same group more than once, you might want to choose a different clue for each game. If not, you may choose to use more than one clue.

9. Be sure to keep the sheets you have used for the present game in a separate pile. When a student calls, "Bingo," he or she will have to verify that the correct answers are on his or her sheet AND that the markers were placed in response to the proper questions. Pull out the sheets that are on the student's sheet keeping them in the order they were used in the game. Read each clue as it was given and ask the student to identify the correct answer from his or her sheet.

10. If the student has the correct answers on the sheet AND has shown that they were marked in response to the *correct questions,* then that student is the winner and the game is over. If the student does not have the correct answers on the sheet OR he or she marked the answers in response to *the wrong questions,* then the game continues until there is a proper winner.

11. If you want to play again, reshuffle the sheets and begin again.

Have fun

TERMS INCLUDED

Henry Louis Aaron

Agricultural

Appalachian Ridge and Valley

Birmingham

Black Belt Prairie

Border(s)

Camellia

Cheaha

Climate

Confederate States of America

Cotton

Counties

Cumberland Plateau

Decatur

Hernando De Soto

Dothan Landmarks Parks

East Gulf Coastal Plain

Executive Branch

Fishing

Flag

Highland Rim

Huntsville

Doctor Mae C. Jemison

Judicial Branch

Helen Keller

Lake(s)

Legislative Branch

Livestock

Longleaf Pine

Manufacture

Mined

Mobile

Motto

Moundville

Nickname

Jesse Owens

Peanut

Pecan

Piedmont Upland

Racking Horse

River(s)

Rosa Parks

Tribe(s)

Tuskaloosa

Tuskegee Airmen

Tuskegee Institute

Union

Voting Rights March

West Florida

Yellowhammer(s)

Additional Terms

Choose as many additional terms as you would like and write them in the squares.
Repeat each as desired.
Cut out the squares and randomly distribute them to the class.
Instruct the students to place their square on the center space of their card.

Clues for Additional Terms

Write three clues for each of your additional terms.

_____	_____
1.	1.
2.	2.
3.	3.
_____	_____
1.	1.
2.	2.
3.	3.
_____	_____
1.	1.
2.	2.
3.	3.

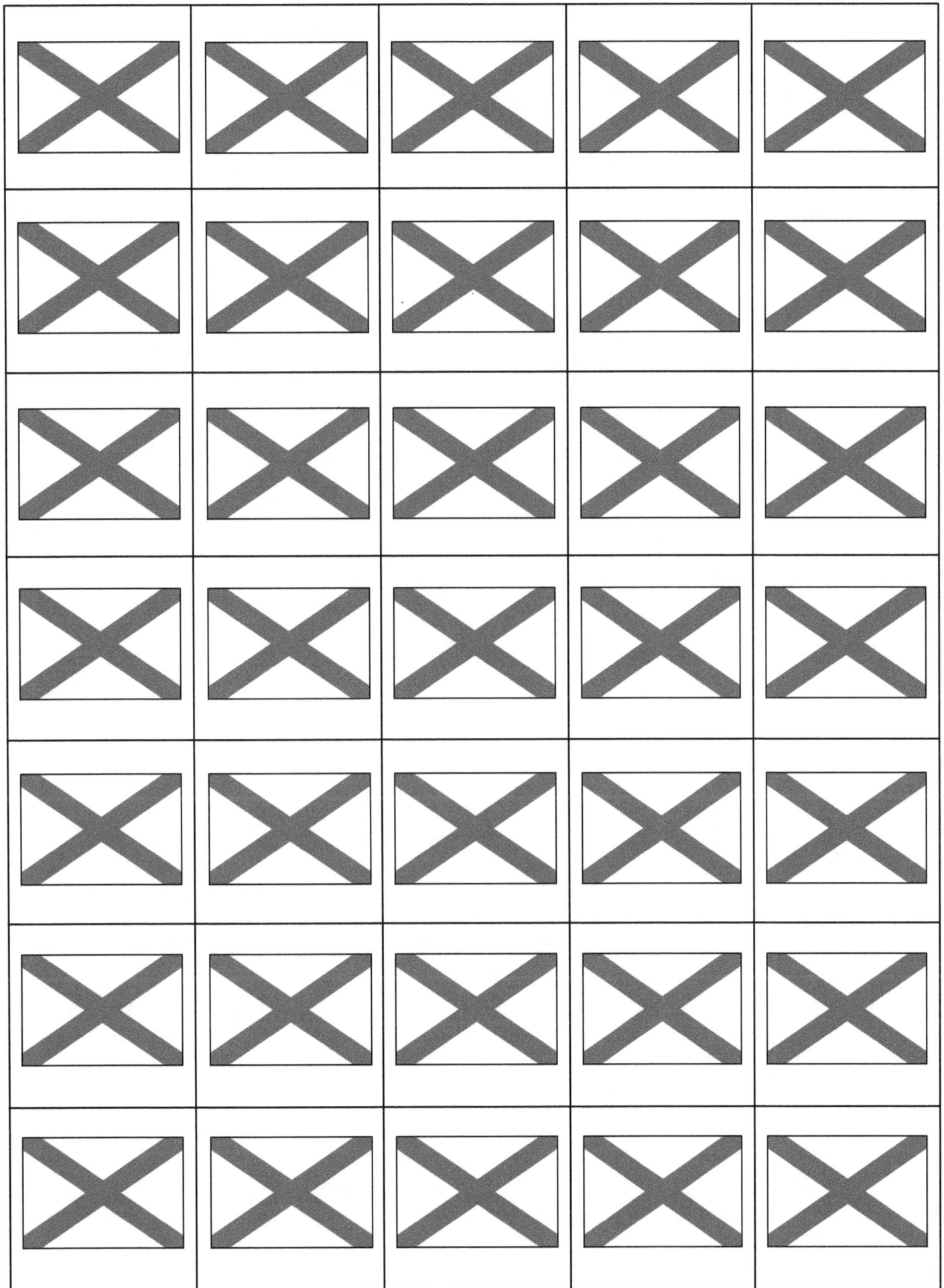

Henry Louis Aaron 1. Nicknamed Hank, this major league baseball player was born in Mobile, Alabama. 2. ___ was inducted into the Baseball Hall of Fame in 1982, his first year of eligibility.	**Agricultural** 1. Top ___ products are broiler chickens, cattle and calves, chicken eggs, greenhouse and nursery products, and cotton. 2. Peanuts and sweet potatoes are also important ___ products.
Appalachian Ridge and Valley 1. The ___ region of Alabama is northwest of the Piedmont. 2. The three ingredients for the manufacture of steel—coal, iron ore, and limestone—are abundant in the ___ region.	**Birmingham** 1. ___ is the largest city in Alabama by population. 2. This city is a major manufacturer of coal, iron, and steel. It was once called the Pittsburgh of the South.
Black Belt Prairie 1. The ___ separates the southern and northern parts of the East Gulf Coastal Plain. 2. The ___ in the East Gulf Coastal Plain was the location of many of Alabama's large plantations.	**Border(s)** 1. These states ___ Alabama: Tennessee, Georgia, Florida and Mississippi. 2. The Gulf of Mexico ___ a small portion of southern Alabama.
Camellia 1. The ___ *japonica* is the state flower. 2. In 1999 the goldenrod was replaced by the ___ as the official state flower; the oak-leaf hydrangea became the official state wildflower.	**Cheaha** 1. At 2,407 feet above sea level, ___ Mountain is the highest point in the state. 2. The name of this mountain in Lineville, Alabama, comes from the Creek word meaning "high place."
Climate 1. The ___ of Alabama is classified as humid subtropical. 2. Although the ___ is said to be subtropical, temperatures in the northern parts of the state tend to be slightly cooler.	**Confederate States of America** 1. Montgomery, Alabama, was chosen as the seat of government for the ___. 2. Jefferson Davis was president of the ___.

Alabama Bingo

Cotton
1. Eli Whitney's ___ gin provided the technology needed to meet the world's demand for___.
2. The boll weevil had a devastating effect on the ___ industry in 1915.

Counties
1. There are 67 ___ in Alabama.
2. The central and western ___ in Alabama are known as the "Black Belt" because of the dark surface colors of many of the soils.

Cumberland Plateau
1. The ___ is sometimes called the Appalachian Plateau.
2. The ___ is northwest of the Appalachian Ridge and Valley region.

Decatur
1. Nicknamed "The River City," ___ is located on the banks of Wheeler Lake, along the Tennessee River.
2. In 1836, this city in Morgan County was chosen as the eastern terminus of the first railroad line west of the Appalachian Mountains.

Hernando De Soto
1. ___ was a Spanish explorer and conquistador.
2. He was the first European to cross the Mississippi River.

Dothan Landmarks Parks
1. ___ is the official state agricultural museum.
2. The museum at ___ focuses on the history of a region known as the "Wiregrass."

East Gulf Coastal Plain
1. The ___ covers the southern two-thirds of the state, except for the Prairie Black Belt.
2. The southwestern part of the ___ around Mobile is low and swampy. The northern part of the ___ is hilly and has many pine forests. This area is often called the Central Pine Belt.

Executive Branch
1. The governor, the lieutenant governor, and the governor's cabinet are all part of the ___.
2. The governor is head of the ___; the present-day governor is [fill in].

Fishing
1. The ___ industry is important. Shrimp, blue crabs and oysters are important saltwater catches. Buffalo fish, catfish, and mussels are important freshwater catches.
2. Both freshwater and saltwater ___ are popular sports in the state.

Flag
1. The official flag of Alabama consists of a crimson cross on a field of white.
2. The red cross on the state ___ is called St. Andrew's Cross.

Alabama Bingo

Highland Rim 1. The area known as the ___ is in the northwestern corner of Alabama. 2. The ___ is also called the Low Interior Plateau.	**Huntsville** 1. ___ is the state's largest city in area but only the fourth largest in population. 2. ___ is nicknamed "The Rocket City" because of its history with U.S. space missions.
Doctor Mae C. Jemison 1. ___ was the first African American woman to become a U.S. astronaut. She was born in Decatur, Alabama. 2. In 1992, ___ flew into space aboard the *Endeavour.*	**Judicial Branch** 1. The ___ interprets what our laws mean and makes decisions about the laws and those who break them. 2. The ___ is made up of several courts, the highest of which is the state Supreme Court.
Helen Keller 1. This deaf and blind author and lecturer was born in Tuscumbia, Alabama, in 1880. 2. *The Miracle Worker* is the story of how Anne Sullivan taught ___ to read Braille and to communicate with sign language.	**Lake(s)** 1. Guntersville, Wilson, Martin, West Pointe, and Lewis Smith are ___ in Alabama. 2. Created by the construction of the Thomas Wesley Martin Dam, ___ Martin is the largest manmade ___ in the state.
Legislative Branch 1. The ___ comprises the Alabama Senate and the Alabama House of Representatives. 2. The ___ makes the laws.	**Livestock** 1. Most of Alabama's annual agricultural revenue is generated by livestock products. 2. The most important ___ products are poultry, cattle and hogs.
Longleaf Pine 1. The ___ is the state tree. 2. At one time, this hard, straight tree was the dominant tree species in the South.	**Manufacture** 1. The ___ of chemical products is an important industry. 2. The ___ of paper products is an important industry.

Alabama Bingo

Mined
1. Bituminous coal, natural gas, petroleum, crushed stone and limestone are the most valuable ___ products.
2. Coal is an important ___ product of the north-central part of the state; methane gas is an important ___ product in the west-central part.

Mobile
1. Founded by the French in 1702, ___ is the oldest city in Alabama.
2. ___ is the only seaport in Alabama.

Motto
1. Translated, the state ___ is "We dare defend our rights."
2. The state motto in Latin is, *"Audemus Jura Nostra Defendere."* It is on the state coat of arms.

Moundville
1. ___ Archaeological Park features Native American artifacts.
2. ___ is known for its Native American earthwork mounds of the Mississippian Culture Era.

Nickname
1. Alabama has no official state ___, but it is often referred to as "The Heart of Dixie."
2. An unofficial ___ for Alabama was "The Cotton State."

Jesse Owens
1. This track-and-field star was born on September 12, 1913, in Oakville, Alabama.
2. This son of a sharecropper and grandson of a slave won four gold medals at the 1936 Olympic games in Berlin.

Peanut
1. When the cotton crop was destroyed by the boll weevil, many farmers turned to this crop.
2. George Washington Carver of Alabama's Tuskegee Institute played an important role in popularizing this crop.

Pecan
1. The ___ is the state nut.
2. There are over 1,000 varieties of ___; many are named for Native American tribes, such as Cheyenne, Mohawk, Sioux, Choctaw and Shawnee.

Piedmont Upland
1. The ___ has highest point in state.
2. Cheaha Mountain is in this region.

Racking Horse
1. The ___ is the official state horse.
2. This animal was popular on the southern plantations because of its versatility.

Alabama Bingo

River(s)	**Rosa Parks**
1. Tombigbee, Alabama, Tennessee, and Chattahoochee are ___ in Alabama. 2. The Mobile ___ Basin is the largest Gulf Coast drainage east of the Mississippi.	1. ___ was born in Tuskegee, Alabama. She has been called the "First Lady of Civil Rights" and the "Mother of the Freedom Movement." 2. She refused to obey the bus driver's order to give up her seat to a white passenger.
Tribe(s)	**Tuskaloosa**
1. The Alabama; Biloxi; Cherokee; Chickasaw; Choctaw; Koasati; and the Muskogee, or Creek, ___ were native to the region that is now Alabama. 2. Many Native Americans were forced to leave Alabama during the Indian Removals of the 1800s. Today the Poarch Creek Indians is the only federally recognized ___ in the state.	1. ___ was a Mississippian chief. He led his people at the Battle of Mabila against the Spanish conquistador Hernando de Soto. 2. He was defeated by de Soto at the Battle of Mabila.
Tuskegee Airmen	**Tuskegee Institute**
1. ___ is the popular name of a group of African American pilots who fought in World War II. 2. When these pilots painted the tails of their fighter planes red, the nickname "Red Tails" became popular.	1. Booker T. Washington founded the ___, which became a major center for African American education. 2. Scientist George Washington Carver headed the Agriculture Department of the ___.
Union	**Voting Rights March**
1. Alabama became the 22nd state in the ___ on December 14, 1819. 2. Alabama was the fourth state to secede from the ___ on January 11, 1861.	1. The 1965 ___ from Selma to Montgomery was led by Dr. Martin Luther King, Jr. 2. The Selma to Montgomery National Historic Trail was established by Congress in 1996 to commemorate the events, people, and route of the 1965 ___.
West Florida	**Yellowhammer(s)**
1. Alabama was part of Spanish ___ from 1780 to 1810. 2. Alabama became part of the independent Republic of ___ in 1810 before it was annexed by the United States and added to the Territory of Orleans.	1. The Northern flicker woodpecker, or ___, is the state bird. 2. Alabama is sometimes called "The ___ State" because during the Civil War a company of Alabama soldiers wore uniforms trimmed with yellow cloth and were nicknamed ___.

Alabama Bingo

Alabama Bingo

Pecan	Henry Louis Aaron	Appalachian Ridge and Valley	Fishing	Black Belt Prairie
East Gulf Coastal Plain	Agricultural	Voting Rights March	Manufacture	River(s)
Union	Longleaf Pine		Nickname	West Florida
Tuskegee Airmen	Racking Horse	Tuskegee Institute	Livestock	Mobile
Moundville	Huntsville	Decatur	Tribe(s)	Helen Keller

Alabama Bingo

Tuskegee Airmen	Union	Judicial Branch	Piedmont Upland	Legislative Branch
Mobile	Hernando De Soto	Cheaha	Racking Horse	Motto
Confederate States of America	Huntsville		Doctor Mae C. Jemison	Tuskegee Institute
Jesse Owens	Peanut	Longleaf Pine	Yellowhammer(s)	Black Belt Prairie
River(s)	Voting Rights March	Decatur	East Gulf Coastal Plain	Tribe(s)

Alabama Bingo: Card No. 2

Alabama Bingo

Huntsville	Tuskegee Institute	Hernando De Soto	Livestock	Union
Mobile	Agricultural	Climate	Henry Louis Aaron	Highland Rim
Racking Horse	Voting Rights March		Motto	Birmingham
Longleaf Pine	Confederate States of America	Moundville	Jesse Owens	Judicial Branch
Tribe(s)	Cotton	Decatur	Yellowhammer(s)	Legislative Branch

Alabama Bingo

Longleaf Pine	Motto	Appalachian Ridge and Valley	Cotton	Legislative Branch
Mined	Camellia	Henry Louis Aaron	Piedmont Upland	Union
Nickname	Jesse Owens		Helen Keller	Fishing
Tuskegee Institute	Agricultural	Voting Rights March	Decatur	Cheaha
Counties	River(s)	Border(s)	Tribe(s)	West Florida

Alabama Bingo

River(s)	Black Belt Prairie	Racking Horse	Cheaha	Cotton
Mined	Tuskegee Institute	Climate	Doctor Mae C. Jemison	Agricultural
Appalachian Ridge and Valley	West Florida		Manufacture	Flag
Helen Keller	Legislative Branch	Pecan	Yellowhammer(s)	Cumberland Plateau
Hernando De Soto	Decatur	Union	Longleaf Pine	Nickname

Alabama Bingo

Birmingham	Motto	Judicial Branch	Legislative Branch	West Florida
Livestock	Racking Horse	Cumberland Plateau	Henry Louis Aaron	Union
Piedmont Upland	Counties		Camellia	Doctor Mae C. Jemison
Decatur	Moundville	Yellowhammer(s)	Border(s)	Appalachian Ridge and Valley
Mobile	Cheaha	Pecan	Nickname	Dothan Landmarks Parks

Alabama Bingo

Pecan	Motto	Flag	Tuskegee Institute	Hernando De Soto
Mobile	Legislative Branch	Huntsville	Agricultural	Mined
West Florida	Fishing		Doctor Mae C. Jemison	Camellia
Longleaf Pine	Jesse Owens	Climate	Tuskegee Airmen	Confederate States of America
Decatur	Cotton	Yellowhammer(s)	Border(s)	Birmingham

Alabama Bingo

Nickname	Motto	Executive Branch	Livestock	Camellia
Mined	Appalachian Ridge and Valley	Piedmont Upland	West Florida	Cheaha
Dothan Landmarks Parks	Cotton		Legislative Branch	Black Belt Prairie
Tribe(s)	Longleaf Pine	Tuskegee Airmen	Counties	Jesse Owens
Voting Rights March	Decatur	Border(s)	Racking Horse	Mobile

Alabama Bingo

Doctor Mae C. Jemison	Hernando De Soto	Huntsville	Dothan Landmarks Parks	Cotton
Counties	Legislative Branch	Nickname	Racking Horse	Motto
Highland Rim	Pecan		Agricultural	Executive Branch
Cumberland Plateau	Black Belt Prairie	Moundville	Manufacture	Flag
Jesse Owens	Yellowhammer(s)	Climate	Tuskegee Airmen	Helen Keller

Alabama Bingo

Tuskegee Airmen	Livestock	Camellia	Piedmont Upland	Dothan Landmarks Parks
West Florida	Cheaha	Henry Louis Aaron	Agricultural	Legislative Branch
Cotton	Motto		Fishing	Confederate States of America
Moundville	Helen Keller	Cumberland Plateau	Yellowhammer(s)	Highland Rim
Climate	Mobile	Judicial Branch	River(s)	Nickname

Alabama Bingo

Birmingham	Motto	Racking Horse	Cumberland Plateau	Mobile
Executive Branch	Highland Rim	Manufacture	Doctor Mae C. Jemison	Henry Louis Aaron
Mined	Legislative Branch		Judicial Branch	Huntsville
Climate	Union	Yellowhammer(s)	Cotton	Tuskegee Airmen
Counties	Decatur	Pecan	Border(s)	Hernando De Soto

Alabama Bingo

Hernando De Soto	Black Belt Prairie	Highland Rim	Livestock	Doctor Mae C. Jemison
Huntsville	Mobile	Appalachian Ridge and Valley	Border(s)	Agricultural
Pecan	Flag		West Florida	Piedmont Upland
Decatur	Jesse Owens	Legislative Branch	Tuskegee Airmen	Mined
Motto	Executive Branch	Cotton	Counties	Cheaha

Alabama Bingo

Cumberland Plateau	Black Belt Prairie	Birmingham	Highland Rim	West Florida
Appalachian Ridge and Valley	Executive Branch	Legislative Branch	Doctor Mae C. Jemison	Confederate States of America
Livestock	Cheaha		Huntsville	Flag
Nickname	Yellowhammer(s)	Camellia	Cotton	Tuskegee Airmen
Decatur	Helen Keller	Border(s)	Pecan	Manufacture

Alabama Bingo

East Gulf Coastal Plain	Legislative Branch	Racking Horse	Doctor Mae C. Jemison	Counties
Cheaha	Pecan	Highland Rim	Agricultural	Motto
Cumberland Plateau	Fishing		Judicial Branch	Climate
Helen Keller	Yellowhammer(s)	Cotton	Camellia	Birmingham
Decatur	Piedmont Upland	Confederate States of America	Mobile	Nickname

Alabama Bingo

Manufacture	Doctor Mae C. Jemison	Racking Horse	Hernando De Soto	Livestock
Birmingham	Judicial Branch	Henry Louis Aaron	Appalachian Ridge and Valley	Counties
West Florida	Pecan		Union	Motto
Decatur	Highland Rim	Executive Branch	Yellowhammer(s)	Cumberland Plateau
Mobile	Jesse Owens	Border(s)	Dothan Landmarks Parks	Huntsville

Alabama Bingo

Camellia	Highland Rim	Executive Branch	Dothan Landmarks Parks	Peanut
Piedmont Upland	Confederate States of America	Flag	Mined	Fishing
Cumberland Plateau	Black Belt Prairie		West Florida	Huntsville
Longleaf Pine	Cheaha	Decatur	Manufacture	Tuskegee Airmen
Counties	Tuskaloosa	Border(s)	Jesse Owens	Motto

Alabama Bingo: Card No. 16

Alabama Bingo

Climate	Rosa Parks	Lake(s)	Highland Rim	East Gulf Coastal Plain
Manufacture	Counties	Yellowhammer(s)	Fishing	Flag
Doctor Mae C. Jemison	Nickname		Tuskaloosa	Executive Branch
Helen Keller	Mobile	Tuskegee Airmen	Racking Horse	Confederate States of America
Moundville	Cumberland Plateau	Hernando De Soto	Livestock	Black Belt Prairie

Alabama Bingo

Dothan Landmarks Parks	Cotton	Cheaha	Cumberland Plateau	Piedmont Upland
Motto	Climate	Moundville	West Florida	Counties
Doctor Mae C. Jemison	Confederate States of America		Lake(s)	Appalachian Ridge and Valley
Black Belt Prairie	Henry Louis Aaron	Yellowhammer(s)	Tuskegee Airmen	Judicial Branch
Tuskaloosa	Highland Rim	Racking Horse	Rosa Parks	Birmingham

Alabama Bingo

West Florida	Birmingham	Highland Rim	Executive Branch	Tuskegee Airmen
Manufacture	Livestock	Motto	Hernando De Soto	Fishing
Rosa Parks	Cotton		Agricultural	Union
Judicial Branch	Tuskaloosa	Moundville	Jesse Owens	Lake(s)
Appalachian Ridge and Valley	Peanut	Mobile	Nickname	Border(s)

Alabama
Bingo

Alabama Bingo

East Gulf Coastal Plain	Rosa Parks	Livestock	Highland Rim	Border(s)
Cheaha	Huntsville	Mined	Moundville	Piedmont Upland
Black Belt Prairie	Flag		Longleaf Pine	Henry Louis Aaron
River(s)	Voting Rights March	Tribe(s)	Jesse Owens	Tuskaloosa
Tuskegee Institute	Nickname	Peanut	Tuskegee Airmen	Lake(s)

Alabama Bingo: Card No. 20

Alabama Bingo

Manufacture	Birmingham	Mined	Highland Rim	River(s)
Black Belt Prairie	Lake(s)	Camellia	Executive Branch	Pecan
Confederate States of America	Mobile		Rosa Parks	Racking Horse
Moundville	Hernando De Soto	Tuskaloosa	Helen Keller	Nickname
Longleaf Pine	Peanut	Border(s)	Climate	Jesse Owens

Alabama Bingo

Alabama Bingo

Dothan Landmarks Parks	Judicial Branch	Lake(s)	Appalachian Ridge and Valley	Cumberland Plateau
Piedmont Upland	Livestock	Union	Executive Branch	Agricultural
Cheaha	Fishing		Pecan	Flag
Tuskaloosa	Helen Keller	Jesse Owens	Henry Louis Aaron	Mined
Peanut	Climate	Rosa Parks	Confederate States of America	Legislative Branch

Alabama Bingo

Camellia	Rosa Parks	Hernando De Soto	Appalachian Ridge and Valley	Border(s)
Birmingham	East Gulf Coastal Plain	Mobile	Manufacture	Henry Louis Aaron
Judicial Branch	Cumberland Plateau		Tribe(s)	Pecan
Confederate States of America	Peanut	Tuskaloosa	Climate	Jesse Owens
River(s)	Voting Rights March	Nickname	Moundville	Lake(s)

Alabama Bingo

Camellia	Nickname	East Gulf Coastal Plain	Rosa Parks	Executive Branch
Lake(s)	Border(s)	Mined	Piedmont Upland	Pecan
Flag	Dothan Landmarks Parks		Cumberland Plateau	Confederate States of America
River(s)	Tribe(s)	Tuskaloosa	Climate	Black Belt Prairie
Tuskegee Institute	Longleaf Pine	Peanut	Livestock	Voting Rights March

Alabama Bingo

Longleaf Pine	Mined	Rosa Parks	Racking Horse	Lake(s)
Henry Louis Aaron	Black Belt Prairie	Manufacture	Camellia	Agricultural
Helen Keller	Executive Branch		Tribe(s)	Tuskaloosa
Union	River(s)	Voting Rights March	Peanut	Fishing
Border(s)	East Gulf Coastal Plain	Cheaha	Counties	Tuskegee Institute

Alabama Bingo

Lake(s)	Rosa Parks	Judicial Branch	Piedmont Upland	Dothan Landmarks Parks
Moundville	Livestock	Executive Branch	East Gulf Coastal Plain	Camellia
Helen Keller	Tribe(s)		Fishing	Longleaf Pine
Climate	Appalachian Ridge and Valley	River(s)	Peanut	Tuskaloosa
Flag	Counties	Racking Horse	Voting Rights March	Tuskegee Institute

Alabama Bingo

Judicial Branch	Cheaha	Rosa Parks	East Gulf Coastal Plain	Huntsville
River(s)	Tribe(s)	Manufacture	Tuskaloosa	Agricultural
Yellowhammer(s)	Voting Rights March		Peanut	Longleaf Pine
Dothan Landmarks Parks	Birmingham	Mined	Tuskegee Institute	Henry Louis Aaron
Counties	Fishing	Lake(s)	Union	Flag

Alabama Bingo

Judicial Branch	East Gulf Coastal Plain	Union	Rosa Parks	Camellia
Huntsville	Lake(s)	Tribe(s)	Piedmont Upland	Fishing
Voting Rights March	Confederate States of America		Flag	Moundville
Tuskegee Airmen	Dothan Landmarks Parks	Mobile	Peanut	Tuskaloosa
Appalachian Ridge and Valley	Doctor Mae C. Jemison	Counties	Tuskegee Institute	River(s)

Alabama Bingo

Lake(s)	East Gulf Coastal Plain	Dothan Landmarks Parks	Manufacture	Doctor Mae C. Jemison
Jesse Owens	Moundville	Mined	Flag	Union
Helen Keller	Tribe(s)		Agricultural	Rosa Parks
Huntsville	River(s)	Legislative Branch	Peanut	Tuskaloosa
Camellia	Executive Branch	Tuskegee Institute	Birmingham	Voting Rights March

Alabama Bingo: Card No. 29

Alabama Bingo

Cotton	Rosa Parks	Piedmont Upland	Doctor Mae C. Jemison	Tuskaloosa
Henry Louis Aaron	East Gulf Coastal Plain	Judicial Branch	Fishing	Agricultural
Helen Keller	Cumberland Plateau		Flag	Mined
Tuskegee Institute	Birmingham	Appalachian Ridge and Valley	Peanut	Tribe(s)
River(s)	West Florida	Voting Rights March	Lake(s)	Union

Alabama Bingo: Card No. 30